RAISED BY THE [M]...
THE CHARLIES DAVIS STORY

Table Of Contents

Foreword

———— ∾∾ ————

"To be a man is to be recognized by the men;"... When the author asked me if I would write the foreword for this book... Needless to say I was honored.

Our lives are all we have. Our legacies are what we leave in our wake. In the meantime, our mission is to discover our purpose.

We are the ignorant, we are the arrogant, we are the misguided. Let us not permit OUT arrogance to further perpetuate our ignorance because we have been so misguided by our life lessons and experiences that we have become wise in our own eyes, amounting to us being so smart that we are actually stupid.

To quote one of my favorite personas..."what we have here is a tale of glory and sin." Admittedly, I am a biter and a writer. Anyone who dares tap into the creative sphere is such, for there is nothing new under the sun. And that right there is the point.

Though I fully encourage you, the reader, to be entertained by the content of this story, his story. I beg of you not to become so distracted that you overlook the lessons and teachings which bring about the genuine meaning of this work. That is to pay homage to History amid providing an awakening to the reader in an effort to do one's part in preventing History from repeating itself. That is the mission. This is our purpose. Influence. The influence of evolution is our legacy. Enjoy!

Introduction

In every neighborhood the world over, there exist the power of an adulterated force referred to as the black hand. Whether seen or unseen, the black hand is the catalyst for the underworld.

What does it take to become the most successful in that world? Simply put, it requires for one to be inhuman. It could prove to be extremely perilous if not fatal for one to visibly exhibit emotions that could potentially expose vulnerabilities that will undoubtedly be preyed upon and capitalized on by the bona fide street predators who occupy that world. To be cunning is to be crafty, which undeservingly has a negative connotation attached to it. Suspicion can be a result of said connotation which begets distrust that causes men and women to become disloyal.

Disloyalty often leads to violence. Violence opens the door for opportunistic power grabs. Hence the initiation of this cycle that has been perpetuated from generation to generation.

Ignorance is poverty; and arrogance without intelligence is hardship. An excessive display of patience in the streets will be conceived as a form of cowardice. Contrarily, one living in that lifestyle absent patience and a plan is imploring residency in the graveyard or the Legal Justice System. The only one equipped to take on a system of unlimited resources is the man or woman who truly has nothing to lose.

WARNING! Nothing to lose and everything to gain brings tremendous power to that one person or group of people who represent that ideology. Nevertheless, for Mr. or Ms. Anonymous;who may be privy to the company of the group, but not to the thought patterns of its core, they are in for a rude awakening.

It was always Southwest

Prologue

Upon exiting the courtroom it was as if the word "GUILTY" echoed throughout the recesses of my skull and off of the walls of the holding cell that temporarily confined my body. My mind, in truth, though I was perplexed I was not totally surprised by the unfavorable verdict. I was aware that the powers that be would assure a victory that would destroy my life as I knew it and attempt to bring my sanity to ruin. The reality was I had been dealing with this corrupt and diabolical system for as long as I could remember.

I feel as if the police in my neighborhood had it out for me due to my alleged street ties to various people in the city. My City. Philadelphia, Pennsylvania. I've been accused of a litany of offenses such as but not limited to gun possession, robbery, home invasion, shootouts with law enforcement, oh, and homicide. Most of which were pure speculation, nonetheless, that didn't deter the prosecution from using it against me in the courtroom in order to portray me as a heartless and calloused beast with no regard for humanity.

Pause. Now don't mistake me for being some kind of saint or law-abiding citizen by any stretch of the imagination. However, let he who is without sin, cast the first stone. Alright then.

All I know is that since entering this holding cell, my mind and my heartbeat have been racing one another in a desperate attempt to catch up with my thoughts as my feet paced in sync with a slow paced rhythm I was unfamiliar with.

"Yo, Cee, what's up? You cool? How did you make out?" Hearing my moniker called, followed by 21 questions, I snapped out of my daze as the individual speaking to me came into focus.

I found myself confronted by the concerned eyes of someone I considered to be a genuine friend. "Oh, my bad. What's up with you, bro? For a minute there I thought you were one of these strangers being nosey.

Anyhow, I'm good, but this situation is all bad! I lost my case and these crackers managed to pull it off using pure deception. To be honest, I expected this would happen. However, if you know me, you know I don't tuck tail and run. I'm exempt from that kind of behavior. Instead I will focus on my get back."

I could tell the revelation of the guilty verdict affected my comrade, because even though he didn't reply to what I told him, his quiet demeanor intensified to an eerie silence. Judging from his body language and non-verbal cues, I knew he was sincere.

Before I was able to truly convince him that I was tayyib (alright), our conversation was abruptly interrupted by other prisoners banging on the holding cell's plexiglass with inquiries of, "Cee, what's up? Charlie, what happened?"

Knowing that the majority of these inquiries were fueled by bad intentions, ulterior motives and hidden agendas, my persona emerged through the wry humor of my fly tongue addressing those nosey ass clowns. "You dudes need to find some scissors and cut out y'all fraudulent concern, because in the real nigga manual it's against the law to be tending to my business without an invitation. My business is reserved for only those I choose to share it with."

At the conclusion of my tirade, my comrade was bent over holding his stomach, laughing. A few others chuckled, attempting to suppress their own laughter. Gradually an appropriate sense of silent contemplation was restored to the scene as spectators began to recognize the seriousness of my spill, becoming more concerned with the peril of the possible outcome of their own situations.

Moments later a Deputy appeared inserting his considerably large key into the lock, opening the holding cell door. After clearing his throat he commenced, "Listen up for your names. This is the go back list. When you hear your name called, approach and give your full name and police photo number (PP No.). If you didn't get into the courtroom today I will tell you what is printed on your go back paper along with your next court date. You will then report to the Deputy down the hall to be cuffed." He proceeded to shout names from the sheet of paper attached to his clipboard as everyone remained quiet in anticipation of hearing their name called. Some with hope of getting back to use the phone, take a shower and receive a late night visit. After about 20 names my government was finally called. Too familiar with this exhausting process, I followed instructions and minutes later found myself along with 32 other prisoners being led to the Sheriffs bus for transportation to our respective facilities on State Road.

Many thoughts ran through my mind during the long drive through rush hour traffic. It all stemmed from the recent turn of events that spawned what was now my fate. Now before venturing down memory lane to my past, my upbringing and specific experiences I've encountered; bringing us up to the false accusations that landed me in this predicament, allow me to say this.

This is a story like no other. Vibe with me as we journey into the realms of adversity, calamity, hardship and despair. My hope is for you to be able to identify with my struggle, if not try to understand why I feel certain circumstances made my fall imminent. Raised by the [M]...

The Charlie Davis Story

CHAPTER 1

My Neighborhood

For those of you who are not familiar with who I am, my name is Charlie Davis, also known to my childhood friends as Cee. I was born and raised in the Southwest section of Philadelphia, in a residential area called Woodland Avenue. This particular section of Southwest is considered by many to be a stand-up section of the city. The history associated with myneighborhood dates back to an era long forgotten, the geographical gang war era. It used to be a place that didn't have your interest if you were not from the area. From the heydays of the gang war era up until the era I come from, the hobby of choice for young, black males was boxing at the Southwest Youth Center; later renamed, the Kingsessing Recreation Center. We took pride in knowing how to throw a right hand. The motto for many of us was that we all acquired a knockout before all else.

There were several boxing trainers who contributed to our fight game. The two I remember the most was a gentleman by the name of Mr. Turner ˉand Old Head Stub. These Two men are responsible for assisting many skilled fighters from my neighborhood with perfecting the art of boxing. At least five made it to a national platform and went on to fight for belts. It was a beautiful thing to be a part of. However, the lure of the streets would cripple most of these men. A plethora a notable hustlers, con artists and gangsters come from this section of Southwest Philly. Some were ruthless and cutthroat, I knew them personally. Others were bonafide bag chasers and some of the realest men in existence, and I knew them all as well.

It's a small area where we all knew each other, and each other's families. That is what bonded us closely together. There's only one school in the area and just about every one of us attended it. That was one of the few places we all met, became friends, associates and in many cases lifelong enemies. This format was in existence generations before mine, and still exist to this very day.

Now that you have a basic fundamental understanding of my atmosphere, I ask that you remain attentive as I walk you further into the lives of myself and a few good people. From the generation before mine. Woodland Avenue produced three handfuls of guys, my peers and I grew up under. You know the select group of men that can be called Old Heads. I can't mention all their names because some live different lifestyles today, but it's safe to say those three letters were in an exclusive category second to none.

Growing up underneath these older guys was a nightmare and a blessing from God. A nightmare because they were predators that thrived on fear. There were body-beatings and vicious tongue lashings designed to break a man's spirit all for the benefit of laughter. These actions were continuous throughout my early years of learning. It became so prevalent that as time progressed, I was left with no choice but to mirror these actions, and **I** grew into character well. If you didn't fight back, things got much worse because they considered you soft. **It** got so bad that I hated to see the Old Heads, but I couldn't prevent it because my neighborhood is so small.

The blessing is that, in a twisted kind of way, everything that happened was done out of tough love and it contributed to who I would become in the streets of Philadelphia.

As fate would have it, the generation before mine took me into their circle and raised me like a little brother and in some cases like a son. Even though I was among them and treated as family, I was reminded on the regular basis that **I** had a place.

In a way I was pushed to the front of my class, but I wasn't ready. So I grew up in that grey area between knowing too much, and not knowing enough.

CHAPTER 2

'Hood is Changing

By the mid 1980's many things subsequently began to change for my peers and I because the generation before us began to change. Their recreational activities upgraded tremendously in accordance with the changing of the times. As for my childhood friends and I, we occupied our time boxing at the recenter, breeding pit bulls and chasing girls. The Old Heads that used to chase us around and punch on us found another kind of endeavor to consume their time and attention; collectively.

The days of pickpocketing, strong armed robberies, snatching pocketbooks, and doing run-ins on the white insurance men were over. In came the epidemic of the drug game. I don't know how it all transpired, but what I do know is that many eyes were opened to a brand-newexperience that could possibly change the conditions of the less fortunate and under privileged.

In the beginning of the coke game in my neighborhood, many of us youngins were forced to sit on the sidelines and watch what we thought was success. This quick change of conditions caused a frenzy and had everybody jockeying for position; all for the love of a fast buck.

Cocaine was the drug of choice being supplied by the big homie and sold by the underlings. Everyone desired an introduction to this product in the hopes of reaping some rewards. My childhood friend and I were not exempt from craving entry as well. But, unfortunately for us, the Old Heads from our neighborhood refused to let us get involved in the activities taking place right before our young and inquisitive eyes. Instead, they would cut us a check and encourage us to stay off the corner.

Speaking for myself, the hypocrisy was baffling. Just think about it, how could someone who was starving just like you, admonish you for wanting a better life in the 'hood? Truthfully speaking, I thought those guys were just selfish. I knew I was fully capable of being competent, but I never understood that theory, and even today I have problems comprehending it.

Having no other option at that time I followed instructions, dropped my head and left the corner. I watched the Old Heads establish themselves in the streets of Philadelphia building impeccable reputations. What started as a leisure involvement in a life of crime, grew quickly into a city-wide movement.

Watching the Old Heads go from selling small amounts of coke to supplying over 200 stones (coke) throughout the city had an effect on all of us in the neighborhood. During this movement certain individuals prospered more than others, but through a collective effort the entire team was winning. This alliance became a structured organized syndicate known as the initials or the triple letter boyz, and history was in the making.

The Old Heads started to set the trends. The days of Lee Jeans and Joe Palmeri were abandoned for Gucci, Fendi, MCM and Guess to name a few. No longer did they walk anywhere, they were coming through the neighborhood in Volvo's, BMW's, Audi's and Pathfinder's. All of their cars were customized with BBS rims, Alpine radios and Gucci interior. Slowly, but surely the movement grew to an unprecedented height. While this transition was going on my childhood friends and I watched, and that caused us to go out in search of our own.

The Jamaicans

By the time 1987 rolled around it wasn't a coincidence that my friends and I chose to dive headfirst into the coke game. Our Old Heads continued to refuse our entry and we'd had enough. We took it upon ourselves to start hustling for the insurgent Jamaican gangs that began to sprout up everywhere. This would prove to be a huge mistake, as well as a learning experience that I am absolutely sure the city will never forget.

For starters, we were naive, and our understanding of the game was very limited. Although we caught on pretty fast, we were being used as pawns for that particular set of Jamaicans. When the smoke cleared and the Jamaicans were forced to go on the run, the Old Heads finally recognized our potential and welcomed us with open arms.

I was first up to go hustle in the green house on Chester Avenue. That house sold $10,000.00 worth of coke every shift: from eight to four, four to twelve and twelve to eight. Unfortunately, we became bored with the arrangement with the Old Heads because they wanted us on post all week, but when it came time to pay us it was a day late and a dollar short. Plus, we were young, wild and reckless so sitting in a coke house all day, every day was not our idea of becoming kingpins. Eventually we quit and started running through the streets.

I had my first brush with the law that year riding in a stolen car. I would later be convicted and sent off to Juvenile Hall in 1988 for a few months. When I was released, instead of • going back to the hood I ended up in Camden, New Jersey with a few friends. We bumped into the Jamaicans again. They were laying real low since the situation back home in Philly. They invited us to their trap with some nice pay and we went back to working for the Jamaicans and it was all love.

Sometime in mid-October of that year I purchased my first car. A 1980, two door Chevy Malibu. I put that car in a crack head's name and when she drove it off the lot for me, I gave her $100.00 and some coke, and I never saw her again. I drove to the sneaker store and bought myself a white-on-white pair of Nike Cortez, a white Fila sweatsuit and a herringbone chain for $450.00. I got dressed in the trap house and headed across the Walt Whitman bridge to Philly. I was feeling myself because I did it my way.

When I got back to my neighborhood, I ran right into one of my Old Heads, Lil Buck. He was 'that guy' in the neighborhood. Dark skinned, short in height, wavy hair and flashy but calm. He was the poster boy for my neighborhood. Anyone that came in contact with him was in awe of his charisma.

Since I was like seven years old, he always called my name two times. When he saw me,he said, "Hey Charlie Charlie. Didn't you get enough of them stolen cars?" I immediately got out of the car with the title and pink slip in my hand to show him I purchased the car with my own money, although I never told him how I got the money. That didn't matter, the car was mine. He smiled and said, "you're up next!" That meant clot coming from him given the fact I used to wear his old clothes.

Arriving at my destination on State Road, the Curran Fromhold Correctional Facility, my thoughts were momentarily interrupted causing me to return to the present and face the reality that awaited me. We were directed to get off of the Sheriffs bus and herded like cattle into another holding cell to go through the demoralizing strip search procedure before changing out of our civilian court clothes back into our county blues. We were then permitted to return to our assigned unit. When I arrived on the unit, all prisoners were locked in for the evening head count and that was perfect for me because I was in my feelings about the sentence I received that day, and I wanted to keep my animal in his cage. As I walked to my cell dudes were banging on the doors, flicking their lights off and on all in an attempt to get my attention, I kept it moving straight to my cell.

As usual it took three counts, one regular, the other a cross over recount, followed by an arm band count before the guard got it right and the count eventually cleared. Immediately, afterwards, two guards appeared at the cell doorto escort me to the hole because of my sentence. I had mentally prepared myself for a long ride and this was part of it. The guards handcuffed me and walked me over to the hole. After entering the new cell, the cuffs were removed and I started to clean the cell, knowing I would be there for however long it took before I was transferred back to the Department of Corrections at Grater ford. I layed down on the bunk, my body was tired and in need of a stretch, but my mind was restless and my thoughts fell back into a state of retrospection.

CHAPTER 3

———— ∽ ————

The Gun

As I tossed and turned throughout the night, images from my past danced around in my head. These images taunted me, so I finally gave in to my reverie. The past brought back memories of me and my guys running through the streets waving pistols without regard. We embraced all of the drama simply because it excited us. We were young, reckless and passionate about our neighborhood. Not to mention we were under the impression that we had to represent the {M} everywhere we went.

The first real war was against the Bartram Village Projects on Elmwood Ave. By this time, we were really into the females and enjoying their sexual favors on the regular basis became an obsession for us. We were attempting to accumulate a high pussy rate to outdo each other for the sake of bragging rights. For me the dark-skinned females always got my attention. One of my first female acquaintances was a pretty, dark skinned, project girl I encountered joy riding in the Malibu. Not old enough to drive, or even have a permit, I was always speeding up and down the street's day and night because I no longer cared about the trap. That car had me off my game.

Anyhow, I met this chocolate beauty who went by Ra-Ra. We talked a while then exchanged numbers. After a few days of telephone conversation, she asked me to visit her. It turned out there was a party going on in front of her building that day. I grabbed my best friend, K.B., and I drove over to her spot hoping to get into a lot more than conversation. Which is exactly what happened, just not in the manner K.B hoped.

Upon arriving to the projects I drove around in search of the party. The projects was lit that day, it *was* a party in front of every building. Needless to say I found her. When I got out of the car I made eye contact with a few guys my age and a lot older. I thought nothing of it because it was a party so I figured everyone was enjoying the festivities.

I found a perch on the hood of my car with Ra-Ra, a few of her girlfriends came over to greet us. Once they were in our presence introductions were made, names were given, and seductive glances were exchanged. About 20 minutes into our little meet and greet one of the females-said, "Oh my God, here come trouble making ass Yotta and them." Whatever-was said after that fell on deaf ears because my focus shifted to the group of guys approaching us aggressively.

Finally, Yotta and two of his homies greeted each female with sarcasm and derogatory comments that were directed at us. In response to the indirect nut shit we gave them hard stares and **I** laughed in Yotta's face. He didn't appreciate that. Yotta asked, "You find something funny, nigga?" So I replied, "You, nigga!" His homie charged at me swinging wildly and we traded punches. When he realized he couldn't get the best of me with his hands he tried to manhandle me, and dude was strong, but I continued to throw right hands and hooks until he let go.

The other two attempted to jump K.B. but were doing a poor job. Before anyone could predict what would happen next, Yotta pulled out a gun. We stopped fighting and backed up to the car but those guys were still getting at us. The girls stepped in between us and that gave us enough time to get our guns from underneath the seat. The projects came alive with petrified screams from onlookers as we let fire erupt from both barrels. That war would last for ten years.

Making it back to the hood we stashed the car and assessed the trouble from a moment ago. The only damage was to the Malibu. Bullet holes were in the windshield and driverside door. Calming my nerves and calculating my next move, I learned a valuable lesson. **I** realized That I made an amateur's mistake by leaving my ratchet int the car when it should've been on my hip. I made a vow to God I would never get caught without it again.

The public disturbance had the streets talking crazy about me. That lil nigga is out of control and trying to be like the Old Heads...etc., etc." One of the Old Heads said, "I wish Lil' Charlie would try that shit with me, I will lay his little as down."... To this day I'm hurt by that statement because it was never for him. However, I've come to realize that my ratchet was meant for anyone that intends to bring me harm. I slowly began to make my mark in the streets of Philadelphia, but it came with a very expensive price tag. My Freedom! And too many enemies to count.

My days and nights were filled with dangerous activities that always involved a firearm. Around this time two of the Old Heads, D-Man and Jama were feuding with some guys- from (The "0") 60th Street, so we drove the Malibu up there. As soon as we pulled onto the street bullets started flying. It got so hot lama had to reverse the block without looking behind him. The Malibu was shot up again. We made it back to our neighborhood and pulled onto Conestoga Street the wrong way. The car was smoking and leaking fluid. When we got out of the car to check the damage another one of the Old Heads, Manny, advised me to move the car off of the block before the police pulled up asking questions, we had no answers to.

After that incident I found my way back to the New Jersey trap. I needed to stack some bread for another car. That Jersey trap was good to me. However, in 1989 the Feds arrested Rain and deported him. P., his partner, went underground and I found myself back in Philly with no real income. Some of the Old Heads no longer viewed me as a kid because of the gunplay, so I was stuck in a grey area between a man and a child.

I ended up on 54th and Regent Street with Rodney "Frog" Carson, who we affectionately called "Beano". I met him through Buck in 1988, right before I went to Juvenile placement. Bucky and I were slap boxing and when we were done, he told Beano I was his favorite youngin from the neighborhood. Beano hugged me and said to Buck, "he's my favorite youngin as well." He gave me his number and told me to call him anytime.

I called Beano a few days later. Recollections of that period in my life remain vivid to this day. Beano acquainted me with living the lavish life. I can remember like it was yesterday; he told me to meet up with him in front of Buck's mother's house. Beano pulled up in the white convertible with the top down after a shopping excursion in Atlantic City. He popped the trunk and surprised me with my very first pair of Gucci sneakers. In that moment in my mind, I began to differentiate what it really was to possess and desire the finer things of this world, as opposed to the tasteless tatters I was familiar with. Needless to say, Beano was an elegant cat.

I started being with Beano at least four days out of the week. We would ride all over the city taking care of our business. There were days when he would drop me off at the Pine Street apartment to pick up $10,000 worth of G-packs for the block. For quite a few months I spent more time with Beano than I did with Bucky. He was always good to me.

One can never thoroughly perceive the demons that may haunt another. When he started using drugs real heavy, I witnessed a side of him the world wouldn't get the chance to see until he became the biggest RAT in the history of the Philadelphia underworld. He's seventy-five percent responsible for the demise of the [M] and its alleged members.

Once I got away from Beano I started being around all the Old Heads again, and Dirty Black became like the father I lost to the streets as a five year old child. He gave me everything a father could give to a son under those circumstances. He supported me one hundred percent.

Unfortunately, my time with him was brought to a screeching halt when the Feds dropped the indictments. I believe we found out they wanted him on our way back from Great Adventures. We weren't surprised, but more or less unprepared for the news that D.B. would have to go on the run. We had been predominately focused on his wife, Big Fs legal affairs. She was out on bail for a Third-Degree Murder charge, and she was at the center of our family dynamic.

Our ride back to the city that day was filled with tension and uncertainty. I am forever grateful that I was able to spend all the time I could with D.B. before he was captured. I swear I cried like a baby when the government took him away from me. I wouldn't see him again until five years later in Philadelphia County Prison after he *was* rearrested on an old murder beef from 1988 and transported from the Feds.

At a time when most people would do or say anything to avoid having to go through what they may have been facing, he was more focused on still being my father figure. He showed me to never allow what I'm looking at to determine who I believe in, as a family member or friend. Those three (3) letters were a gift from my Old Heads and a curse when the government took them away. I guess it's safe to say, when you remember what you've done, you can't forget who you are.

CHAPTER 4

———— ⁓ ————

The Jake is Back

One afternoon I heard a knock at my mother's front door. When I answered it I was taken aback at the sight of my Jamaican homie, Rain, all smiles posted out front with a brand new foreign idling in the middle of the street. He informed me that he had been back in the States for a couple of months, and he wanted me to help him take back the New Jersey trap, Of course I obliged. As we drove over the Walt Whitman bridge into Jersey, **I** asked Rain how he made it back so fast? "No country can hold me." was his reply.

When we pulled up to the trap spot some other coke boyz were coming out and staring hard. I reached for the strap and Rain grabbed me and said, "no guns". Imagine my surprise, because "we're always ready to burn some skin" was his motto. In any event, we got the spot back and I immediately went to work rebuilding. I stayed in Jersey for the next three weeks with Rain checking in on me and dropping off the work.

One evening I slipped across the bridge to Philly and I went to P.W.'s house after checking in with my mother. We started flexing on each other about our sexual conquest. Eventually I decided to call a few females to entertain the guys. After several conversations with various women I dialed Ra-Ra's number, the project girl. It rung a few times before she picked up. Our conversation started off with her telling me about all of the rumors she'd heard about the street activities. I changed the topic right away and got into some other kind of dialogue. In no time my mind became clouded with lust thinking about her moistness and I ceased seeing clearly.' I asked her if I could come through because I wanted to see if she could back up that titillating tongue of hers. She said yes, so I told her to have a friend for my homie and she agreed. I hung the phone up and told P.W. what it was.

On the way we laughed and joked with some people we passed by in the neighborhood. As we approached the projects I took the strap off of safety and headed towards her building. Since she lived on the first floor I could look right into her window. I saw no movement, which I thought was strange considering when we spoke a short time ago the background sounded alive. I knocked on her front door anyway. She answered, but only cracked the door. I tried to look in but I couldn't see anything because it was dark. I asked her if I could come in and that's when she slammed the door on me.

For a second, I thought she was playing until I heard P.W. call my name with alarm in his voice. I stepped out of the building and Yotta stepped out of the shadows armed with a machine gun. They had the drop on me again but was doing too much talking. Consequently, I took advantage of the opportunity at redemption and started shooting through my coat pocket before pulling it out and letting the entire clip ride. Yotta was hit three times that night and I was hit once.

As we fled the scene some project dudes played good Samaritan and tackled P.W. They held him until the police got there. I made it back to the neighborhood, but when I looked up my block the police were already at my house. I went to a friend's house around the corner and asked him to go and investigate what was going on at my house. When he returned, he informed me that the police were claiming that I killed someone that night. I called Rain to come get me and he drove me to a hospital in Jersey to get treated for the shot I took in the foot. Yotta lived, P.W. went to jail, and I went on the run. I stayed on the run until the end of 1990.

For about six or seven months in 1990 Rain and I were getting to a heavy bag in Camden, New Jersey. He purchased a 500 Benz, his partner Pete purchased a BMW. My other homie Sheed got a Toyota Creseda and I grabbed **a** gray Mustang with a Pioneer stereo systemin it. I had every color Fila sweatsuit, an Italian linked gold chain and bracelet to match, and everything else a young kid my age could want.

The craziest thing happened to Rain. One day we were counting money and the next thing I know big bro was spitting up chunks of blood. When he left the house I never saw him again. I would later find out that he died from full blown AIDS in 1991 while I was away doing a bid. **I** hope he is resting well because that was a live ass Jamaican.

CHAPTER 5

―᷈᷈᷈―

24 Hours after the life sentence

The first few hours after the life sentence I was in my feelings, but after the first night in the hole I was just an angry motherfucker thinking about the way those people treated me in that courtroom. The next morning,I woke up and wrote a few letters to some people who I thought could assist me. Next, I pulled out my pictures for motivation. I started getting that nervous energy I feel before any situation, so I started to pace back and forth in the cell.

As fate would have it, I received a visit from my little sister. When I saw her face she broke down crying. I greeted her affectionately putting on my best face, attempting to assure her that it would be alright. That made her even more emotional. As she tried talking through sobs I continued assuring her. Eventually she snapped at me saying, "Nigga, them crackers just gave you forever and a day and you're talking about everything is going to be alright. What about us? Your family? You're too G'd up..."

I interrupted her in mid-sentence and said, "Sis, I love you and appreciate all that you do for me, but I need for you to understand that the battle is not over. It's only round one. I would like to think that you know me. I won't give up without a fight to the very end!" We continued our conversation with me telling her who to get with because I needed a sack. **I** had to run it up for the lawyer tab.

Back from my visit with my little sis I resumed pacing back and forth in the cell contemplating this up hill battle, because giving up in defeat was not an option. My mind wondered 'aimlessly to the challenges that lie ahead of me. Unlike my previous oppositions whom I beat with audaciousness and violence, my new competitors were more powerful, more conniving, and their resources were unlimited. I knew I was in for the fight of my life, I thought so much for so long I exhausted myself and I had to rest.

When I awoke from my sleep, I replayed everything that happened in the courtroom and I genuinely felt robbed of my life. I had to ask myself some hard questions. Did I have a team of strong supporters? No, Did **I** have the 530,000.00 needed for an appeal? No. Is there another option? No. The goal is to remain strong, come what may. **I** was always clear about that rule.

CHAPTER 6

———✦———

D.O.C. Bound

As I expected, I was awakened one morning around 4:00 am and instructed to pack up my belongings. I got up from the metal bunk and prepared myself for the inevitable strip searches and questions, then more strip searches and more questions. I was escorted to the receiving room of the county jail and placed inside of a holding cell. Minutes later I was interviewed by a nurse for any medical concerns. I replied no to all of her questions. Shortly after the sheriff deputies arrived. I was searched, handcuffed, and escorted to the sheriffs van for my trip back to the Department of Corrections as a LIFER! During the ride I slipped back into my reverie.

I believe it was 1987 and Jay-M was 17 years old, fresh out of Cornwell Heights Juvenile Placement Center. He wore a green Troop sweatsuit and gold Alpina glasses. All my big brothers and Old Heads were there, most of whom would later become the core members of the

[M]. We sat on the bench in Kingsessing playground talking, boxing and enjoying each other's company. Who knew that we would never do it again without the letters dictating it. Jay-M and Bucky were cousins, and Jama was his younger brother. We all grew up on the same block and our grandmothers lived directly across the street from one another. They were always a part of my life, so as natural progression would have it, I was raised by the [M].

The summer of '87 my Pitbull, Cherry had a litter of puppies, and they all possessed distinct features. All of the puppies were born with colorful eyes and no tail. When they were old enough, I carried them from my house to the playground for the Old Heads to see. I had twelve pups and ended up selling ten of them for $300.00 a piece, I walked home with $3,000.00 in my pocket that day. I gave my mother half of the money and purchased a scooter and a dirt bike with the other half. The playground was the meeting spot for everyone in the early days of the M. I loved those times because no one was too important to stop by the park.

My mother would often stop by the park to check on me, even though she knew I was safe in that setting. She would only lose her cool when **I** was in the streets with the Old Heads. My mother was well known for her show up and show out behavior. Although she knew all of them, I was still her little boy, and at times she felt I was growing up too fast.

At the time we lived right behind Gump. I could <u>walk</u> out of my back door and walk into his house. His cousin, Goob lived around the corner from us. B-Bop and Fat Mus' mothers were like big sisters to my mother. Black Magic, his nephew R.M., Bucky and Quiet Storm all lived within ten houses of each other. Tall Bucky, Peezo, Neal and Mont lived two blocks up from us. We were **a** family long before the drugs, the guns and the alleged murders. We were a family long before those three letters.

I heard the sheriff honk the horn snapping me out of my reverie. We had arrived at Graterford State Penitentiary. I began to gather my wits and prepare myself for the humiliation of the next round of strip searches, as well as the intrusive questions. I can never get used to strangers asking me personal questions designed to assess my thinking patterns solely for the benefit of a threat assessment. So, I'm sitting in the intake area with 25 other prisoners waiting to be seen, I'm going to be here all day. I retreat back into my head.

Man-Child

I was that scruffy little boy in the neighborhood that your mother warned you to stay away from. I was poor and we were on welfare. My mother is a woman who doesn't care for the material things in life, that's how I was raised in her home. I don't know if she brainwashed me to think that way because we were broke or she went through some kind of transformation along her journey in life. All I know is we had very little. So I learned early on to go out in the world and get the things I needed for myself.

I was eight years old when I started shoveling snow with the older boys in my neighborhood and shortly thereafter I was packing grocery bags at the neighborhood supermarket. I would carry people's groceries to their houses for one dollar. In the very beginning I had problems because I was the youngest and the smallest, not to mention I wasn't that bright. Some of the lady customers would see the older kids running in front of me to get the job, they would turn them away and call me to assist with their grocery bags. It was a woman who told me I needed to get more aggressive if I wanted to make money for myself, after I carried the groceries to her car she gave me two dollars, a kiss on the cheek and told me to stop letting those older boys bully me.

Since I was a young kid it has always been the woman who inspire me the most! They have been my best friends and my worst enemies, starting with my mother_ She has been into the church since I can remember, even while partying at the neighborhood bars, she was so complicated to me as a child. She never wanted me *to run the streets, so when she caught me with the older crowd she created a scene right there on the spot. However, when we got home she would go right back outside to the bar. At times there was no food to eat in the house, at other times there was no heat in the house. I started to realize that my mother was a religious fanatic, she would always tell us God was going to make things better but it only got worse.

I started to rebel against her authority very early in my life because I would go to my friend's house and see more than one television set, video games, but most importantly it was warm. I knew from an early age my living conditions were not right; My mother sometimes called my sisters and I into the house to preach about Jesus Christ and the church while steady sipping on beer and smoking a cigarette, I would act like I was listening, when I had enough I would tell her I was going to bed. However, I would climb out of the back room window into the abandoned house next door and,run the streets all night. I *always* came back with money to feed my sisters.

It was around this time I figured out my mother's husband was a bum and a drunken coward who wasn't carrying his weight around the house. However, when I began to produce for the household, he became really aggressive toward me, I now understand he saw me as competition instead of help. He was the reason why my mother was in the streets making scenes about me hanging around the older crowd, because it was <u>him</u> that thought I was learning too much too fast. I was almost nine years old when I started swinging back and attacking him with a knife. My mother would always tell me to listen to what he says, I'd always respond the same way, he is not my real father. When I couldn't take it anymore, I would run to my mother's twin brother and he would beat the shit out of my mother's husband. She wouldn't speak to me for days afterwards. That was fine by me because I would come and go without any problems. would go to the corner store where Quiet Storm worked for his grandfather, and he would give me free food to sweep the floors and wipe off the video games. When Neil's mother opened her store around the corner, he also gave me what I wanted, These are the guys the city would fear as the Junior Black Mafia. We were a family before the letters.

CHAPTER 7

―――⚍―――

The Women

All my life the women were my riders. In the streets and especially in the prison system. My mother has always been there for me the best way she knows how no matter the circumstances and her teachings pulled me through some real tough situations in these places. Her theory about materialism not having no real meaning in life has always separated me from people as a whole. Yeah, I like expensive clothes and a nice watch or two, however, when I had those things I never worshipped them like I've seen so many do, because my mother taught me that those things didn't define my humanity.

When I bought new clothes, she would take them out of my room and give them away to her husband and his friends, when I got bent out of shape she would just laugh at me. I thought I was doing something brilliant when I was selling coke and spending all the money on clothes, but all she saw was her eldest son being a basic street guy with no real understanding of life. The only way she could reinforce her lessons was to rob me of the things I had begun cherishing too much. She literally expressed this to me. So, I say thanks to my mother for not allowing me to become a basic hood guy. My power as a free man and a prisoner is the result of women thinking for me, because I was a fool. I honestly thought I could run through a brick wall and still survive. Everything I know about peaceful living is the result of the women showing me the way.

When I was broke the women gave me the money to buy the coke I sold to get back from financial affliction. It was the women that put my cars and apartments in their names. It was the women that bought me clothes to look presentable in the courtroom. It was the women that reassured me that being different was a good trait to have. It was the women that introduced me to places outside of the trenches. It was the women that hid me from the police all the time. Itwas the women who pointed out the snakes in my circle, using only their intuitive nature. It was the women I had the deepest conversations with. And it was the women I wronged in the end because I was too arrogant to know when I was being ignorant, and too ignorant to know when I was being arrogant.

That's the story of my life, falling to utilize the talents all the women seen in me. It was my mother who told me I was a kind hearted gangster and that was a dangerous trait to have if I let it go unchecked. It was a women who told me I trusted my friends too much, and that would ultimately be my downfall. It was the women who told me when I was being manipulated by another woman. I believe we meet people for a reason, good or bad, there is a reason for us crossing paths. The women have been, and continue to be great teachers to me, all emotions included. The good, the bad, the ugly and the indifferent. The vindictive reactionary behavior, and the jealous hearted paranoia is something I will always find comfort in because that's raw emotion. That emotion allows me to learn the true lessons of love and hate. The women made me realize my worth because I can never compare myself to a woman, I have no need to compete with them. Which means I can accept them as they are, opinions, views, values as well as experience.

I've befriended many different kinds of women. The loudmouth ghetto chick with no filter and no sense of danger. These were the women who always told me the truth because they didn't know how to hide behind fancy words, their world was right there in front of me. Now the street chick is an entirely different animal because they know many different men. in the city, in EVERY city! Their company came with a check most of the time, it didn't matter if you were paying for the information, or the opposition was paying her regarding your whereabouts. Eitherway money and favors were exchanging hands. The street chick is about her money. On the other hand I've witnessed real street chicks stop wars, because they knew all parties involved. Just think about the women who have kids by made men in different parts of the city, the experience and knowledge those women bring to a circle of men. A real street chick can connect one hundred different men all over the city with a few phone calls, that's real POWER! POWER is relative, not absolute.

As a child I always found myself doing things I had no business doing. I ran through old and abandoned houses; I fell from trees. I had bottle fights that almost cost me an eye on more than one occasion. However, this particular day I was at the neighborhood swimming pool with R.M. I was probably nine or ten at the time and he was thirteen or fourteen. I decided to do a back flip off a ledge into the water. Luck was not on my side that day and I hit my head on a sharp edge, busting it wide open. When I regained consciousness people were gathered around me checking to see if I was alive. As I sat up, R.M. and my mother were clearing a path through the crowd for the paramedics. All stitched up, I found my way back to the swimming pool the very next day after being released from the hospital.

Before the close of the 1980's RM. would be indicted with the [M]. According to urban legend R.M. smuggled a gun into the Philadelphia City Hall courthouse and found a seat next to the loved ones of a particular RAT who was testifying against someone from the [M] with the weapon in his hand. Rapper Beanie Sigel recreated that moment in the movie State Property as his way of paying homage to the audacity of the men.

Lincoln Drive is a curvy road in the city. One-night Black Magic decided to navigate it by steering with his knee while relighting some weed that Pezzo had just passed him. My heart sunk into my stomach as I held onto the handle attached to the roof over the back door while riding behind the driver's seat in the Black Acura. Gump was sitting next to me laughing at my nervousness. We were coming from Magic's house in the West Oak Lane section of Philadelphia. We'd been there all day eating, talking and watching Italian mob movies. The movies where they actually spoke Italian, so we had to read the captions off of the television screen. I loved Magic's house, even though I'd only been there twice. To have a quarter of a million dollar home in the eighties was a big deal, especially in my young mind.

As I'm sitting in the intake area of Graterford State Prison, a prison worker recognized me from the picture in the newspaper. He spoke to me and started shaking his head, he said "your Old Head Jay-M thought you were going to beat those charges." I replied to him, "can you get` him down here?" He said, "let me try," and a short time later Jay-M walked in smiling. Although I had talked with him on the phone it was the first time I'd seen him up close since the indictments from a couple of decades ago. We hugged, we laughed, and we talked legal strategies. Then a cop car pulled up on me to inform me I was going to the hole because I was separated from a guy I stabbed at another prison years earlier. I was crushed because I needed more time with my Old Head. We hugged and said our goodbyes, then I was escorted to the hole.

I did the whole strip routine once again. By the time it was all over I was angry and exhausted. When I finally got to a cell I just laid down and drifted off to sleep

When I awoke I went back into my head. I started thinking about the case that caused me to get my first state bid. As rumor would have it, I was in the act of committing a crime, when a Philadelphia Police Officer attempted to intervene, depending on who is telling the story. A shootout ensued and one of the police officers were hit. To this day I haven't seen any evidence of that nevertheless that's how the government maintains it all happened. Still a juvenile at the time of theshootout with the police I was charged as an adult and given a ransom bail. I didn't have it so I had to sit down until I could figure out how to get myself out of that predicament. However, there weren't many options available to me at the time. I sat in jail for about one year give or take a month, until one day I was speaking with another juvenile prisoner. His attorney told him about a program that assisted juvenile offenders with bail. At least that's how the guy explained it to me. I contacted my court appointed attorney and relayed to him all of what I heard;**I** even gave him the other lawyer's name. He promised to investigate the matter and get back with me. Well, a few weeks passed, I heard nothing from my court appointed attorney so I called him again. I received no answer. Maybe a week later I received a legal visit from the court appointed, he was all smiles when he sat down. He said you are going home in a couple of weeks. He said it was no such thing as a program that paid for juvenile offenders bail, but he filed a motion under Rule 1100e. Basically if you were in confinement without stepping in a courtroom for one hundred eighty days you were eligible for some form of relief. I received house confinement and was back on the sidewalk within weeks.

CHAPTER 8

Before the cop shooting

It was 1992 and I was just coming home from an eighteen month bid in the Cornwell . Heights Juvenile Facility. I was back in the city and moving around like I never left. I was home for three weeks, when a guy by the name of Pee mistook us for someone else driving a Blue Impala. Some words were exchanged, and it turned into a heavy shootout. He had something big and with a lot of fire power because it seemed to shoot forever. I was beside myself with anger, I felt like he won the battle. So I paid M-Dot the master car thief to steal me a car. I rode around every day for a week until I spotted the car from the shootout that night. It was around 4:00 P.M. and still daylight outside, I pulled right next to the guy and to my surprise he was on point. We started firing upon each other at close range. I let off at least ten rounds and he was giving it right back. I hit the gas, dipped a few corners, blew a couple of lights and parked the car. To this day I have no idea how we missed each other.

A few days later I'm driving down Woodland Ave. and I stop at the red light on 55th street. As I'm sitting there waiting for the light to turn green something caught my attention. I see • the Brothers from the Nation Of Islam standing in formation around my friends S.G. and Fly-T, but the scene didn't look right, so I blow the light in an effort to get closer. That's when I see it all take place, the brothers did a smooth kidnapping. One brother accompanied Fly-T in his cherry • red Cadillac Allante, instructing him to follow a handful of his compatriots in the vehicle ahead of them. The remaining brothers escorted S.G. to another waiting car bringing up the rear, which would be utilized to box in Fly-T in route to a place from whence they probably would have never return. I was familiar with the tactic because I had a brief run with some of the brothers in the Nation. I caught up with them about two blocks down and cut them off. I hopped out with an eight shot riot pump shotgun and told the brothers that my friends weren't going anywhere with them. The brothers' eyebrows and facial hair were shaved, they looked like death angels just staring at me. I cocked back the gun and told the brothers we can all die tonight. They chose to live to fight another day.

As a reward for intervening on their behalf against the brothers they gave me access to a small portion of their money and all of their guns. I never knew they had it in like that until they let me in the immediate circle. It's ironic because S.G. was tied into the [M] through

Manny and O. He was still carrying that flag I loved so much, he even purchased the exact same color car

Beano had to give the neighborhood that feeling and reminder to never forget the ones that came before us. Fly-T was everything his name represented. However, by the end of that year the Feds were back in my neighborhood with their sights set on S.G. and Fly-T. We were all getting ready for a trip to Virginia Beach, but I wouldn't make it because we got into a situation and the police chased us down. I ducked Off into a back alleyway alley tossed my pistol but the police got it and me. They also found two other guns that belonged to the guys. The police told me, "We know these guns are not yours but you are responsible for the high crime rate in this vicinity". I was sick to my stomach; I knew it was a wrap for a couple of years. I kept my mouth shut and did the bid. I know the guys would have done the same for me. That's one thing I will always champion, keeping it tall!

A few months after my arrest a friend of mine came running to the cell I was housed in and said, "your team is on the news". I ran to the T.V. room, and sure enough I see Fly-T's bright green BMW station wagon, with the headlines major cocaine bust. The Federal Government labeled Fly-T as the youngest cocaine Kingpin in Philadelphia history. S.G. escaped the indictment, literally! He went on to become a manager and music producer, getting acts like Philly's Most Wanted and Beanie Sigel signed with music labels.

CHAPTER 9

———— ⌇ ————

Me against them

The prison environment is mentally draining. If a person is not careful it is easy to fall victim to the petty jail house politics. Sometimes I look into the dayroom and wonder which one of the prisoners I may have to murder? As well I think to myself, which one of these prisoners will kill me? I see men falling apart every day, it scares me. I've seen men upbeat and laughing one day, the next day I see them talking out loud about God trying to kill them. Then you have the man who becomes more violent and unpredictable because he has lost his mind. Those guys began thinking everyone is talking bad about them to others. That paranoia makes them lash out and that creates massive tension in the surroundings. It is very easy to be pulled into someone else's mental break from reality because we are stacked on top of each other. If a guy is having a mental melt down, someone else may perceive it as a sign of disrespect and that may be cause to put the knife in the air.

So, we have to become many different things in here and a psychologist is at the top of the list. We have to do a threat assessment everyday to see who is still with *us* in the realm of reality. Sometimes I look into the mirror and I do not like what I've become. Sometimes I don't recognize my very own voice, because my words and action are designed to see if I'm talking to the same guy I was talking to previously. I feel disingenuous, I feel like I'm being deceptive, but I justify it as a survival tactic. I'm aware that most guys in this environment have very little support from the outside world, if any at all. More often than not people in these places are support driven. If a guy feels he is loved on the outside it is more likely that he will approach his life in here with a bit of diplomacy, because he is trying to hold his support net together. On the other hand if a guy feels he has nothing to lose, he will have a reckless disposition and that attitude is very infectious. When you have bitterness, jealousy, arrogance and most of all rampant ignorance in a tight space, you have a recipe for the ultimate disaster. I have to protect myself at all cost. This is a situation that I have to face head on, there's no escaping it.

I'm living my life in a fishbowl. I have-to act like the whole world is watching when I address an issue, on the same token I cannot let the onlookers dictate how I move. If I overreact to a situation and over gas someone with overwhelming force I become the stupid nigga that hasn't learned from my previous mistakes. However, if I don't go hard enough the onlookers will say I've grown soft, eventually that will lead to misplaced energy. Basically, doing something to someone who didn't deserve it. That gives people even more to talk about. So I lose no matter how it ends. In life a cautious mind is sometimes more dangerous to your wellbeing than it is to your overall aspiration to win; because a cautious mind is wired to think and thinking sometimes creates fear and doubt, which leads to hesitation and mistakes. However, reckless abandonment is a fools approach to every issue. I guess it's safe to say that timing is everything. But, trial and error is the only method I know. Although that has robbed me of a substantial part of my life, nevertheless, I will never shoot myself in the head to kill the man standing next to me.

CHAPTER 10

In My Head

As my childhood friends and I built upon the legacy of our neighborhood, the Old Heads united dynasty fell apart into divided factions, with hidden agendas and ulterior motives. This caused everything and everyone around me to crumble into tiny, little pieces. A power struggle had taken place right before our eyes. Older guys in the family started to plot the demise of each other because of greed and paranoia. When the government was closing in on the [M] the Old Heads became reversible turn coats, pointing the finger at who they thought could become a potential government witness. First, there were the sit downs, second, there were the fist fights that resulted in people masking their true feelings. When the clouds finally opened up to rain, the dark and wicked intentions became clear.

There were three incidents that changed the overall atmosphere in the neighborhood. Nineteen eighty <u>nine</u> and nineteen ninety, would take my old head Neil. Neil was originally from Jamaica, but he was adopted by Woodland Ave. before the coke era. He *was* a beautiful dude with a smile that could light up an entire room when he walked in. His family owned one of the neighborhood grocery stores and we all called his mother "Mom"; Allegedly Neil was called to meet someone in the Richard Allen Projects (The Island), in the North Philly section of the city to squash a beef. He was led to a dark building and murdered on the spot. My other Old Head, Hick, was hit multiple times but survived. He would later become a Rat. While he was in the hospital we all were going to visit, I heard him say him and Neil were set up by someone close. He would never say a name but he was really paranoid. He told me to never trust anyone in the family. He would later repeat the exact same statement in his mother's living room after he was released from the hospital IN FRONT OF ALL OF THEM! I was young and still oblivious to the trust factor. Years later his words would ring true in my ears like a catchy tune. Treachery is the element I least expected.

As an adult I now understand why the show of strength was short lived. There was a shadow in the dark pulling all the strings. That person was cutthroat, jealous hearted and had ruthless ambition. Because of Neil, we the younger generation were given the green light to wave the pistol on anyone from North Philly attempting to set up drug operations in our neighborhood. We followed those instructions for four years after Neil was murdered. People who was not in that eight's circle from our neighborhood could never understand why we kept getting at them guys. We had some vicious shootouts with the Island

and Penntown projects, all because someone was attempting to hide their treachery from the hood. When I was old enough to understand what was going on it was too late the damage had been done and I had to stand on the drama. Old beef from yesteryear is only good if one truly understands the history behind the beef. Anything else cannot be justified.

Back from memory lane I'm confronted with the harsh reality of "life in prison". Just the thought of being kept behind the fence/wall forever is a pain so deep, so uncomfortable, I feel like I'm having a heart attack. The thought of a strange white man asking me to see my entire naked body whenever he feels like it has me questioning my sanity. The thought of never again being intimate with a woman is a feeling that is indescribable! Having no freedom to choose whether you're coming or going is spiritually draining. I'm going back into my head. Let's finish the story...

The next incident was Lil "E" the brother of a known family member. Even though he was not originally from my neighborhood we loved him just the same. Lil "E" was the smooth ladies man and the sneaky type. Every time we crossed each other's path he always gave me hug and called me family. One night he got into a car with some guys who were allegedly from North Philly and was found dead the next day. That pushed everyone over the edge and multiplied the paranoia beyond repair. The pain I saw in his brother's face that morning on Conestoga Street is something I will never forget. He was ready to kill or be killed... But the chaos was not over.

Because of the plotting, suspicion and paranoia I witnessed the Old Heads form clicks amongst themselves. I won't name who was in what click, but it's safe to say the division was real and to be honest now that I look back on things I believe it was always like that. The illusion was the united front. How could anyone imitate such craftiness?

CHAPTER 11

Bucky

After the loss of Neil and Lil B, the entire city of Philadelphia was brought to its knees when our most beloved and respected Old Head was assassinated! The city was moving slow that day in May of 1990, but our hearts were bleeding fast because Lil Bucky was the cornerstone of our neighborhood! I've never seen the city openly mourn a person the way he was mourned. His funeral was like a Mummer's parade on Broad Street. It's something we expected for a man of his character. As the story goes, someone waited outside of his house on-Creighton Street in the

West Philadelphia section of the city, and as he was putting the key in the door he *was* shot multiple times. I will never understand why he was killed because everyone that I've ever known loved the man, he was always the voice of reason. I can remember a few months before he was killed, his daughter's mother rammed her car into his on Woodland Ave. We picked up bottles and bricks preparing to do some violent things to her, but he cussed us out and told us to stay out of the domestic beef. That incident taught me how to distinguish the difference between the street issues and the domestic ones.

At his funeral I walked up to his casket, I thanked him for the experiences he had shared with me, I promised him I would hold the hood up at all cost before anything else. I then told him, I love you Old Head. I couldn't hold back the tears and as I walked away from the casket I broke along with the rest of the city.

On the hills of Buck's death the streets of Philadelphia turned into a war zone as rivals double sided against each other. No one was safe. The movement that was so powerful two years prior had crumbled into pieces of treachery and despair. Shooters were on a murderous mission inspired by revenge. The sentiments were to remove anyone who was thought to have participated in the conspiracy against Buck. He was the voice of reason, now that he *was* gone blood was being spilled without a second thought. People were directing shooters to hit their personal enemies and disguising it as revenge for Buck. There were guys stepping up pretending to restore order, when, in fact they were attempting to manipulate others with the illusion of power. They were the ambitious types with no real talent. In that atmosphere we all paid a price. I lost my Old Heads and the neighborhood lost its security blanket. Some good men went to prison, while other good men went to the graveyard. So many hearts were broken and so many relationships remain shattered to this very day. There are secrets layered with deceit and more secrets regarding who shot Buck. With all the conspiracy about who did what and why, I'm just honored to have known such a beautiful character!

Back on jail time! After forty five days in the hole I was released into the general population at Graterford, apparently the prisoner who I was separated from left the prison. I hit the law library hard and when that was complete I was insearch of a way to generate lawyer money for my appeal. However, when I began moving around the prison I was truly disappointed with the environment. Guys were mentally broken, bitter and lost somewhere in the nineteenth century. I could not believe the mentality in that prison because it is so close to the city of Philadelphia. After a few hard pressed ideas, I came up with something that worked for me in a short period of time. I managed to put away six thousand dollars before the inevitable happened.

One morning I was walking back from the law library and a guy asked me why I was looking at him? I responded "I'm notlooking at you, I'm looking past you" as you can imagine the guy didn't like that, so he said something disrespectful. Heated words were exchanged followed by jabs and hooks from all angles. Things didn't go in his favor, so he ran to his cell to get his knife. When he started running towards me with it in his band; a childhood friend of mine passed me his knife. The guy and me proceeded to stab each other viciously. When it was over his nose and ear were hanging off of his face. I was bleeding as well from the head and shoulder. The cops stormed the block, we were taken to the medical department to get patched up. I went to the hole and he was air lifted to an outside hospital.

CHAPTER 12

─ ✹ ─

Towards The End Of An Era

The last time I'd seen everyone in the same place was at Buck's funeral, the mood was tense, there was a heightened sense of paranoia because the Feds were snapping pictures and none of the Old Heads trusted each other anymore. I'm not sure if Old Head Quadir was there, even though he lived around the corner from me I never knew him on a personal level. However, I did see Al. he is another one I didn't know on a personal level. When **I** was around him it was in a family setting and he was in daddy mode. When **I** was leaving the funeral **I** seen the "Do that brothers" driving that Pathfinder jeep with the bullet holes in the windshield and a few others.

Nevertheless, that's when I started seeing Chris "Light Skin Chris" Anderson driving the cars and barking orders like he was a boss. **I** never understood how he became apart of that circle. Just six months prior he was smoking crack and stealing guys drugs from underneath the car tires. Chris, was a pretty boy who was known for fighting and getting the ladies, he was never a gangster. So it was no surprise when he flipped and became a government witness against the Old Heads. Chris, *was* one of the guys standing on the sideline with stars in his eyes when one of the Old Heads would show up and show out. Chris, would go on to become the biggest RAT in the [M], along with Beano! He destroyed multiple families with his over exaggerated Mafia tales. He wasn't around them for a long time, but he testified against them as if he was there from the very beginning. I honestly believe he was a plant by the Feds and for the Feds.

He single handedly generated a lot of attention to the circle when he sucker punched the referee at the summer league basketball game at Myers Playground. The referee happened to be a prison guard with connections to law enforcement. Chris, began to flex his muscle, he became extremely arrogant because he was under the impression that he was untouchable until hesquared off with Mont. Mont was one of the best fighters in the Old Head circle. Chris invited him to a fair fight and was punished from the beginning to the end of the fight. Up next it was Sugy-Pooh and Huck's turn, it went real bad for Huck. Sug, beat him into submission, even though Sug is from North Philly, we love and respect him in my neighborhood as family. After the indictments dropped "Huck" became a government witness. Then there was the scuffle between Jay-M and Quiet Storm. That hurt my young heart. Just like the incident between Jay-M, Jama and Magic. Then I watched Gump absolutely dominate Fat Juice. I was begging Juice to stop fighting but he wouldn't give up. Tall Buck and Peezo fought as well but that wasn't fair because Tall Buck sucker punched Peezo when he didn't expect it.

The Junior Black Mafia has always been my family and I didn't know life without them, I'm truly grateful to have been Raised by the [M] because I wouldn't be who I am today without that experience. The good, the bad, the ugly and the indifferent. Our friends give us strength and that makes us vulnerable, because we are trusting them with our lives more than anyone else. Even if we don't trust them one hundred percent, we are still trusting them. That trust places them in a position to hurt us directly and indirectly, hence the saying careful who you chose as a friend because we are often judged by the company we keep. As we grow, we should want to give ourselves an advantage by choosing the friends that will assist us with building opportunities that will give us the edge in life instead of giving us away to our rivals (The System) through arrogance and stupidity.

Light Skin Chris, did all that talking and still received forty years in the Federal prison system. Life is unfair but that doesn't mean our friends should be. Knowing that makes life more dangerous because we will need to make an informed decision that could possibly affect our happiness. Acceptance is not easy but sincerity is. We don't adjust to the environment; we make the environment adjust to us. Fake men are the heroes in all of their stories because they've broken all the rules and need a reason to justify their inherent weaknesses. I wish the Old Heads could have seen. Chris the way I did, a pretty boy crack head that lived off of women. The end of an era... I'm going back into my head.

CHAPTER 13

After The Cop Shooting

Days after my release to home confinement to await my trial for the shootout with the Philadelphia police I was right back at the streets. While I was gone R.M.'s brother, Doc, had suffered a loss to a guy twice his size and the guy attempted to capitalize off of it by teaming up with the North Philly guys we were at war with. Together they attempted a takeover and were almost successful; I finally saw the guy after four days out of jail and I flashed the pistol on <u>him </u>in broad daylight. I chased his car up the block ˈlaying my best to end it but that 178 was just too fast. I tucked the gun, ran through the neighborhood playground and disappeared into a back alleyway. A few days later the guy reached out to a few of the. Old Heads from the [M], the ones who escaped the indictment. They asked me to leave it alone, the guy apologized and left the block.

Around this time I met a beautiful girl from the neighborhood. I was at her work place ordering food when she made a comment about my attire; we exchanged numbers and a few other things and I fell in love with Jazz. She was fun to be around and whenever I wanted to share her space she allowed it without any questions. She had the biggest hazel eyes I ever seen, every time she looked at me with them I just wanted to protect her from the entire world, especially the world I was a part of up until that point I had never met a girl that soft. She never raised her voice at me, but when she spoke it all made sense. She would be the reason I slowed down for a few months. During this time I had a trap house in the vicinity of 60th street doing very well, my gun was warm and life was good until it wasn't.

I was involved in a high speed car chase trying to duck the police task force. I crashed the car, jumped out of it and went on a light weight foot chase before it turned into something else.

The police claimed I attempted to fire upon them again, however, they claim my gun jammed. That's their story! But it's kind of hard to believe because I had two automatic weapons with four clips on me that night.

A couple of months before I met Jazz I was riding through the projects looking for a lady friend, when I pulled to a stop in front of the building I asked a few guys that were standing out there if she was around. A guy asked me my name to which **I** replied "you clowns know my name, its Lil Charlie". The guys started reaching for their guns, I went to get out of the car and Jim grabbed me by the arm, he said "no Charlie lets go". I didn't even have a gun, I was so arrogant and full of myself because my name was real colorful in the street that I thought they wouldn't shoot. As I'm pulling away from the building I see through the rear view mirror a car pull to a stop in front of the guys I was just talking at and they were pointing in our direction. The car came speeding up behind me firing shots. Non-Stop bullets were coming through the trunk, the back seat, and the window. I was hit in the head, T.B. was hit in the back and they tore my friends car to pieces that night because of my arrogance.

At the hospital that night the detectives attempted to question us, but we didn't have anything to say. I stayed in the hospital for twenty four hours before checking myself out against the doctor's orders. All I had in my mind was the get back. I found out from the streets it was Yotta that did the shooting, I came home from the hospital my head still swelled up like a basketball, I grabbed the pole and went through the projects waving it until it was empty.

For an entire month I didn't let up on the projects; I drove through there, I rode a mountain bike through there, I even walked through there one late night and did something. I could never catch that guy. Anyhow, the guys kept asking me to slow down because the police were asking too many questions but I couldn't comprehend their reasoning. One night I was in my feelings and I went through the projects in my personal car and did something. I didn't put the car away afterwards and that's why the task force attempted to pull me over because they were looking for the car. I moved on pure emotions and it cost me my freedom. I wouldn't see the streets again for another seventeen years and nine months because I couldn't control my emotions.

After I *was* processed in the jail my first phone call was to Jazz, as soon as I said hello to her she began to cry. I felt as if I somehow failed her. She kept saying I love you, over and over again. I assured her of my love as well before the phone was disconnected. As the days turned into months in the county jail I was up to no good, fighting, stabbing, I was involved in two jail house riots that resulted in me being re-charged for a guard's nose being broken. I was transferred from one county jail to the next and back again, all while my Jazz stayed loyal to me. She even took a second job to assist with the lawyer fees. I went to trial for the two guns first, I was found guilty on every charge except pointing the gun at the police. Jazz wrote a letter to the judge, in addition to speaking on my behalf in open court. Because of her support I received just twenty four months on those charges. The very next day I was called to the receiving room at the county jail, where I was met by two Philadelphia Homicide Detectives. They logged me out of jail and transported me to the Philadelphia Homicide Unit, located at the police headquarters on Eighth and Race street. When we arrived there the detectives handcuffed me to a chair and left me there for the better part of that day. Finally they interrogate me and its about the guy I had the car to car shootout with. The detectives scream, yell and do all that clown stuff. I said nothing except I want a lawyer. I then asked them to drive me back to the jail because Jazz was supposed to visit me that day. I didn't get back to the jail until later that night. Those people were talking about death row and all I wanted was the girl.

MARCH 11, 1993 **PAGE 13**

Ex-JBMer gets break for his help

Info against cohorts brings jail reduction

by **Jim Smith**

Daily News Staff Writer

Rodney "Frog" Carson lived in the fast lane while selling drugs for the murderous Junior Black Mafia in West and Southwest Philadelphia.

Carson once testified that he earned profits in excess of $500,000 over a six-year period, blew the easy money on "fine cars and clothing" and jewelry, "and things of that nature," and had children by three women.

His testimony at three trials helped put a number of leaders of the drug gang in prison for life. One convicted JBM boss, Aaron Jones, recently was sentenced to death for a murder.

Yesterday, the 26-year old Carson learned his reward for assisting federal, state and local authorities in the successful prosecutions of more than a dozen JBM leaders, members and associates.

U.S. District Judge Marvin Katz sentenced Carson to a three-year prison term for conspiring with other gang members to sell more than a ton of cocaine in Philadelphia between 1986 and 1991.

Since Carson has spent the past 2½ years in custody, he'll be out of jail within six months, living with a girlfriend and their son under an assumed identity far away from Philadelphia, with security provided by the Federal Witness Protection Program.

Carson, who pleaded guilty to drug-trafficking charges, had been facing a prison term of at least 14 years, said Assistant U.S. Attorneys Allison Burroughs, Abigail Simkus and Joel Friedman, prosecutors in the Organized Crime Division.

His testimony against the JBM "was critical to the successful investigation and prosecution of numerous defendants," prosecutors wrote in a memorandum to the judge, recommending leniency.

"He has done everything a cooperating witness can do," and was "worthy of the court's mercy," defense attorney Robert J. Marano told Judge Katz.

In an apologetic speech to the judge, Carson called his former JBM pals "advocates of the devil."

"I gave my all to help atone for what I've done," added Carson.

"...All I want to do is rid myself of the crimes that I have committed. By speaking ... of it I have become a better person ...

"I was proud to take the stand and testify ... I made it through all the death threats." ■

Inside the Drug-Dealing Empire That Ruled West Philly | Flashback | OZY

By Seth Ferranti

The Daily Dose JAN 10 2018

WEST PHILADELPHIA--Junior Black Mafia lieutenant Leroy "Bucky" Davis, a 22-year-old former amateur boxer, was murdered at

2:30 a.m. on May 14, 1989, while attempting to enter a row house on Creighton Street in West Philadelphia. He was coming home from a party with a girl he hoped to bed but got aired out before he could pull his gun out of his ostrich-skin boots. The hand-picked successor of JBM street boss Aaron Jones, who was locked up and facing a litany of charges, Bucky had been tasked with running Southwest Philly while Jones fought the cases against him. (CNBNewsnet image files)

Although no one could have predicted it, Bucky's murder would set off a chain of events that upended the organization that had ruled Philadelphia's inner-city neighborhoods since the mid-1980s with a terrifying ultimatum: Get down or lay down. Which basically meant buy cocaine from the JBM or deal with the consequences. It was a slogan that the federal government claimed epitomized the ruthlessness of Aaron Jones.

With a combination of brawn and business acumen, Jones ascended the criminal hierarchy.

Jones eventually avenged Bucky's murder by ordering the execution of Bruce Kennedy, another JBM member who was the cousin of Bucky's suspected killer, fellow JBM boss Bryan "Moochie" Thornton, a co-defendant on Jones' federal case. Kennedy was dating Neisha Witherspoon — Jones' baby mama — and the incarcerated Jones was not pleased. Someone had to pay for Bucky's death, and it might as well be the man who was nailing Jones' girl. Street justice, some might call it. On Aug. 18, 1990, Jones' men carried out the hit.

CHAPTER 14

———— ∾ ————

The Streets is Talking

As a young boy being raised by the [M], I was taught to respect the streets and to disregard the police inquiries into any and all criminal activities. However, not everyone received that kind of training. Two months later the Philadelphia Homicide Detectives were back with even more information about something else. I was transferred to the homicide division once again. As soon as I entered their unit all of the detectives stood up and started clapping for me. I was placed in a cell and handcuffed, then forced to wait for hours before anyone attempted to interview me. Once again I requested my attorney and once again they tried that good cop/bad cop routine. Only this time they wanted me to listen. The detectives had almost all the information about my movements in the streets. I was shook to my core! When I left homicide the second time I was not so cocky, I was really paranoid. I didn't know who to trust. Where did they get that information from? How did they know that? Who was talking? And why tell on me? I always played by the rules. What I've come to realize, there are no rules in the streets. People. give the police information when it benefits them in one way or the other. People become informants to get out of jail, people become informants to get loved ones out of jail. As well people become RATS because it's the only way for them to retaliate against a more powerful adversary. I didn't know what was happening? I did know I was afraid for my life. It's so strange, the neighborhood is with you when you're free and winning. On the contrary, when you're locked away and it appears that you are never going to be free again, everyone will disassociate themselves from you. Often times our greatest obstacle is our naivete. There is no such thing as loyalty. It's a rumor!

Sometimes the love may be real, however, self-preservation is the strongest pull when it comes to human desires. When someone tries to hurt us, we fight or we run in an attempt to preserve our life. It's no different at the homicide unit **or** in the courtroom. What a person allows himself/herself to be reflects what principles they represent; it has nothing to do with loyalty. It's the personal constitution of the man/woman that will control the outcome of his/her behavior patterns in the face of legal opposition. If a person loves their name, and their image that is sometimes enough for them to face the prosecution head on because that's that persons personal constitution. On the other hand if the person has no self constitution to protect they are susceptible to a demonstration in the box. (On the stand)...

By the time my second trial came around I was a bit more serious. Experience made me more conscious of the system as a whole. I prepared myself by reading the discovery and familiarizing myself with how to select a jury. I was under no illusions, I knew it was a hard case to win. After I picked the jury, they were sworn in and the trial commenced. No one was in the courtroom except my mother, my old head and a few childhood friends of mine. However, no one wanted to be associated with the attempted murder of a police officer, so I was found guilty five days later, sentenced to a minimum of twelve years six months to twenty five years on the maximum. I was shipped off to prison with no fan fair, just me and all that time. I wasn't yet twenty one, all I kept thinking was how the fuck am I going to do all this time?

CHAPTER 15

———∽∾———

Prison Life

I've spent many years in and out of one facility or another and for the most part they are generally the same. The juvenile camp, the adult prisons, the mentality is predatory in nature, whether it's the typical tough guy behavior or the more sinister deviance, its all the same. I've managed to find my way in the worst prison conditions because I don't mind punching or stabbing. For the most part violence is the acceptable norm in a prison setting, but that approach has come with the harshest discipline the prison has to offer. I've spent years in solitary confinement, I was placed in the Special Management Unit, the Behavior Modification Program and countless other jail house experimental programs designed to monitor my behavior patterns. I was placed in the program because people in the environment chose to rub me the wrong way instead of petting me. Most of my problems are the result of my name preceding me, when people hear my name with a negative connotation attached to it before they actually meet me they are on edge. One wrong look, one wrong gesture can become a major problem. Then there's the prisoner attempting to create a name and image for himself by misusing another man's name. It can become tiresome to maintain a level head in such a manipulative environment.

The staff members are no different. I had a problem with a particular sergeant at one of the jails. Every couple weeks he would stop by my cell and say to me, "your not so tough Inmate Davis", and **I** would ignore him every time, the more I ignored him the more aggressive he became with his words. Until one day I had enough and I responded by calling him a racist.

Coward, he issued me a Misconduct report and claimed I threatened **to** kill his family. I was escorted to the hole, later I was found guilty of all the charges by the hearing examiner (jail house judge). He gave me a long speech about my troubled history in the Department of Corrections and how I was such a problem, when he was done I explained to him the charges were fabricated, I also informed him that I was going to punish the sergeant for manufacturing the misconduct report against me. They chose to disregard my warning even after telling me how much of a problem I was.

I was released from the hole two months later and the next morning I punished the sergeant on the walk. I was given an emergency transfer from that prison one hour later, but before I was transferred a State Trooper read me my rights and charged me with assault on a prison staff member. I did take the case to trial, however, on the day I was to pick a jury the District Attorney for that county offered me two years, so I coped out. During that entire incident I was starving for ten days, the guards cut off the water in my cell and would only cut it on every two days and destroyed all of my property. It didn't matter that I ignored the guy for months before it turned physical, all people cared about washow it ended. That is how most people see it when looking at someone else's life, the ending! Most are not concerned with the chain of events that brought about a particular ending. I have always been judged without people knowing the full details of the story. When I attempt to express the truth and correct the misinformation people don't appreciate it because the illusion is more exciting to embrace, that is what people see when they see me, an illusion.

When I see my reflection in the mirror I do not see what the streets see because I know the real person. Those years in the hole, in silence gave me real strength, all men and women should judge themselves at their worst, only then can you fortify your essence.

When the war with the guards was over I requested to be released from the hole into the general population in that prison, the request was denied and I was transferred again. About nine months had passed but the Department of Corrections was still in punishment mode. I arrived at another prison and was greeted by the Security Response Team (S.R.T.); they were clad in all black, bullet proof vest, riot sticks and shields. They escorted me to their hole and were attempting to provoke me the entire way there. I ignored their over dramatized show of strength. I made it out of that hole and to the general population shortly thereafter, but in three months I was transferred again because the security department found an old separation. I went through three more prisons because no other jail would accept me into their general population. I was filially released from the hole after my family and friends contacted the State Rep. and a very special senator. Once I was released I thought I could settle down and stay away from the hole, that was not to be. The security department was sent to search my cell two times a week, every time I walked off of the unit I was pulled over and patted down aggressively. I noticed the other prisoners steering clear of me because they didn't want the administration to associate us. One day I awoke on the wrong side of my jail house cot and decided I wouldn't be going for the bullshit that day. I vowed to break someone's face if my cell was searched or if I was pulled over for a body search, I was tired of the harassment. I walked to the inmate dining hall received my food tray and sat down to eat. Another inmate offered me some condiments which I accepted and while I was eating the meal a guard walked up, told me to dump my tray and get the fuck out of his dining hall. I continued to eat my meal, other prisoners were begging me to walk away without a fight, when I got up from the table to leave he followed me calling me a slow asshole and I hit <u>him</u> with a right hand, followed by a left hook and he went down. When I attempted to stomp him another guard jumped on my back, I slammed him off and ten more came. I tried to fight them all but I had no win. They dragged me away to the hole handcuffed and tired. They maced me, beat me with the riot sticks and broke my leg. They cut my clothes from my body while I was still handcuffed and threw me into a dry cell. (cell without running water, no bed etc.), it would be days before I received any medical attention. The guards and I went at it for another six weeks before things started to calm down, they attempted to train me to face the back wall of the cell with my hands on my head to get a food tray. I would laugh at them every time and I would go hungry another day, I started losing weight really fast but **I** was determined to be treated with some dignity and respect. It worked and the guards no longer sabotaged my food trays, I proved my point, I'm the matter that matters. Back to the story...

CHAPTER 16

The old heads of our old heads

The gun fights and territorial battles grew increasingly epic. We were at it with different sets and a rare thing happened that caused my team and Ito double down. We went to war with a more advanced group of gangsters who were the old heads of our old heads; guys that were legendary in our neighborhood two generations before ours. Everyone that was not part of that beef sat wide eyed and with open ears as they cast their predictions on how the rivalry was going to unfold. It all started because our old head "Gleek" had to punish one of the guys from the old head's group, they came back and tried to jump Gleek and when that didn't work they murdered him right there on the block in broad day light, to make matters worse they hit a six year old little boy. That child was related to Magic, R.M. and Doc. While the police were attending to the crime scene on our block we hopped on the motorcycle and drove up to the old head's block and fired upon them. Like all the other wars, our approach was sight on scene. Every time we bumped into the old heads it was game time. We were hiding in the bushes outside of the neighborhood bars with new age semi-automatic weapons and dropping twenty to thirty rounds on them every time. In return them old heads were firing off them revolvers like nobody's business, I learned real fast why they were legends in the streets.

One day I came home to find one of them sitting in my living room and smiling like the cat who ate the canary. I reached for my gun but my mother stepped in front of me and told me to put it down right in front of the old nigga. She asked me to leave it alone because they were her childhood friends, I agreed but I wasn't happy and neither were the guys. She made an O.G. call and I had to respect it. That brief intermission of peace lasted until I was arrested on a weapons charge. About a month into that bid I called home and the *guys* told me they had to drop one of the old heads because they started drama all over again.

1 believe that's how it happened because it never really ended the first time. My friends thought they were on the run for murder, however, the Old Head didn't die, he survived two shots in the face and lived, he lost an eye but never did he say anything to the police. That Old Head was back in the streets and looking to get revenge a few months later. I would find out later on in my life that some of those same Old Heads held me in their arms when I was a baby. I salute all Woodland

Avenue Legends!!! There was a powerful presence that surrounded us at all times, the spirit of real men!

It was always the Old Heads from one of the generations ahead of us or ahead of the ones before us that got involved when we did something to someone because they were the only ones that could talk to us, they were the only ones who knew how to talk to us. People are into the streets for many different reasons, some people are forced into the streets because of necessity, while others are attempting to be a part of something to establish an identity for themselves because they're empty inside. And yet, others are born into life with no foreseeable options. There have been many wars, shootouts and a lot of hurt in the streets, I could have been the victim on the end of someone's barrel if the Old Heads didn't protect me. I'm sure I've disappointed them somewhere along the way, because they've disappointed me at a particular time or two in my life. Nevertheless, I was fortunate to have the [M], as well as the generation before them guide me to safety, a victory or a resolution, even the ones that were strung out on drugs.

I can truly say the advantages I had in the streets were due in large part to the friendships that I've developed over the years. Those relationships are a direct link to the [M], because without them I wouldn't have known the streets as intimately as I did. I have forever been loyal to a fault, that has caused me more pain than actual joy but I do not know how to be anything else. That's the story of my life, give more than I receive, and hope people will love and respect it enough not to shoot me in the back of the head. Let's finish the story...

CHAPTER 17

Anyone can be an informant

When I was finally released back into society after serving close to two decades in prison, **I** came home on the heels of a major Federal Indictment. Most of the people who were arrested were close friends of mine and others were people I met along the way. One of the persons involved was someone whom I trusted, loved and respected, that person would ultimately become the most important informant of that indictment; and I was delivered from prison straight into her awaiting arms!

After being on the streets for maybe two months, I drove to North Philadelphia to see the Old Head, he asked me who was in my car. I responded with her name and he responded with "isn't that the girl on Glasses' indictment?" I said "yes that's her", he gave me a very strange look and asked me to never bring her to his block again. He asked me, "why she was not locked up in the Federal Building?" I responded, "she is on the streets because my man in the Feds cleared her name." He shook his head 'NO" and said that doesn't sound right. I thought he was being overly paranoid, he asked me to drop her off, come back and have a talk with him.

On my way to drop her off to her mother's place she kept asking me about him. **I** didn't respond because **I** thought she too was being paranoid. I dropped her off at her mother's place on City Line Avenue, and I drove back to North Philadelphia. When I got back there he was waiting on rne. He started to tell me how the Federal Government works. He told me that most people are arrested and released after they sign a contract to become Confidential Informants. **I** listened to him for twenty minutes or so without interruption. I assured him I understood the lesson but I didn't believe she had taken that route. I shared what I knew of her street history as we continued to talk, we came to an agreement that I would never bring her in his presence again. He asked me to remain on alert and to watch for any anomalies in her routine, I assured him I would do just that. We parted ways and I was deep in thought the entire way back to her mother's place.

When I arrived there I sat in the car for sometime thinking about this woman possibly being a Confidential Informant. As the days, weeks and months went by I noticed that she was always on the phone with my man in the Feds they were laughing, cracking jokes and moving along like the best of friends. I thought everyone was standing tall. When I would attempt to send <u>him</u> money through her she would say people don't want us communicating but then I'd mention the frequent phone calls and she would agree to do it. When I read the indictment and questioned them about certain things that sounded suspect they would tell me a story of some kind. I would ask, "what could I do to make things better", and they would brush me of as if they never heard me offering my services. I would feel uncomfortable around her sometimes and at other times she was more thorough than the guys I had around me. She was more reliable, she seemed trustworthy, and always ready to assist with any new endeavors. On the other hand the guys seemed lazy and distrustful of anything outside of their circumference. Naturally I gravitated more towards her and that was the biggest mistake I ever made because it is the reason I am serving a life sentence. The relationship was riddled with infidelities on both sides, by the time I was arrested we had grown miles apart from one another which is why it was so easy for her to fabricate the story she gave to the police, or failed to correct the story that they gave to her. Once I was arrested everything came out into the light, she was an informant and had been an informant for at least two years prior to my release from prison. I was thrown right into a shark tank, I never stood a chance. Love is replaceable in the face of self-preservation.

I understand why so many people double cross each other. I disagree with a lot of the situations I know of personally, only because I understand it's an ignorant mind attempting to play politics. Although those politics are empty and underdeveloped it's nevertheless a game of dirty hood politics. Some Rats are under the impression the government works for them because they move against people based on information that they provided, that's justification for weakness. I've sat in this cold and lonely cell many nights thinking of the signs I chose to ignore from that woman because I was still living in the past. I was taught men lead by example, that has always been successful for me but it wasn't relevant to her at that time and I felt she was not at all receptive to it. When we would have conversations she would always justify ratting as a strength. She would say things like, "I don't judge people, we all have secrets", she would say "No one lives by that real stuff anymore"! She was talking that way because she was a working informant and she had to validate her decisions to turn people over to the government.

I can remember being in the supermarket with her and she spoke to two guys that looked like they were government officials. When we made it back to the car I asked her did she know those guys in the funny looking coats, she said No. But I swear those guys were looking at me as if they were studying my facial features. Maybe a year after my arrest I bumped into her codefendant on the Federal case at the county jail. He explained to me he had a disc from his legal discovery that showed the woman in question talking to him on the cell phone in front of the Federal agents and they were tracking his phone through her. That's how he was arrested. After our conversation I learned he was at the county jail because he was testifying against someone who was on trial for murder.

The fact that my significant other was an informant for so many years blindsided the streets. Even when people thought she was an informant my presence wouldn't allow them to voice it because they knew I would defend her name with my life. That was the perfect cover for her to move around the city. Everyone of her co-defendants on the

Fed case flipped on each other and became government witnesses, by design or otherwise. I ignored what was right in front of me the whole time and **I** felt it! Never confuse a kind act as love. Respect maybe, but love is a stretch too far.

The guy in the Feds knew she was an informant the entire time however he never revealed it to me because he needed her to perform in the world, **I** assume. My mistake has been a lesson, it has humbled me and I've gained the confidence to listen to that inner voice, make the connection to the people around me No matter how they attempt to disguise the shape of their manipulation. I miss the days of my childhood where ignorance was bliss and I had the Old Heads.

CHAPTER 18

———✦———

Before the Murder Charge

I was the proud partner of an Auto Mechanics/Body Shop. We bought and repaired cars that were involved in accidents. We would then sell them for a profit. It was a good business that generated a nice revenue stream, as well it kept me off of the streets and away from trouble. I enjoyed the business of fixing and selling cars because I was constantly moving around dealing with so many people from different walks of life. One day I'm on the phone talking with someone about a specific paint color for a certain car and the next day I'm on the phone with someone about a particular car part I wanted for one car or the other. The car business is a lot like the drug game, it's constant action and the people are looking for ways to save a buck or two at your expense. There are shady mechanics in the car business, there are scammers in the car business as well, it's a cutthroat business altogether, but that's why I enjoyed it, because it felt like that energy and excitement I used to get from the streets. Everyone had an angle to separate you from your money.

The shop was the hang out spot for us. All the players in the city would come by the shop to speak with one of the guys or me. I was receiving a lot of business because the shop was cheap and I was trustworthy. You didn't have to worry about someone stealing from your car, stealing a part off of your car, or placing a device on your car. We just did the work without any of the trickery. When people were looking for a car we would allow them to sit with us at the shop while the auction was going on and bid on the vehicle themselves. That way it would never be any disputes about the cost of the car, the repairs, and we didn't want to get stuck with a car that was unsalvageable. So even if you ordered the car and we couldn't fix it, it was still your car. A legitimate business that kept me in the street loop was something that I adored because I wasclose to it without actually being all the way in it. I was sure to have my freedom for years if I kept moving like that, but it was all a dream. Just six months later it would all come crashing down around me when a team of agents raided my shop with a warrant for my arrest.

I was speeding up the highway in the SS trying to beat my parole agent to my apartment in Chester, Pennsylvania. He called and requested I meet him there for an unscheduled home check. I pulled up to the complex and took off my Rolex placing it in the glove box. I then popped the trunk to switch the Gucci sneakers for the 2011 Air Max. I ran in the apartment to perform a few minor adjustments and waited for him to show. Finally, he knocked on the door with another agent at his side, we greeted each other, and he proceeded to do the home check. When he completed the search of my apartment, he requested that I submit to a urine test. I complied and the test was negative for any drugs. However, he wanted to have a talk with me, he said "some people are concerned about the expensive clothing you've been seen wearing", I informed him that I was gainfully employed, and he gave me a sneaky smile and replied, "be careful". The parole agent left, and I peeked out the window to make sure he was gone. When I made it back to the car I grabbed my watch, turned up the music and mashed the gas back down the highway heading towards Philly. He'd just informed me that someone called the Parole Office one me.

I knew whoever called the parole agent was either scared of me or jealous of my progress. It didn't matter because I'd come to realize the rules of the game had changed in my absence. It was a brand new wave and instead of using force to win against an opposition, people were becoming rats. They would find what they thought was a weakness and exploit it however they could. It's not unfathomable this has been going on for years. It's not a new generation type ofthing because there are rats from every generation. Some generations may be more accepting of the practice than others, nevertheless people have been cooperating with the government for years. If someone has offended my code of honor I blame that person, not the generation.

CHAPTER 19

The streets is cold hearted

After six months of freedom I was still ignorant to all the street politics in the city. I kept asking why no one had addressed the lost of my childhood friend and kept getting the run around about my homie "B" from the Blumberg housing projects in the North Philly section of the city. I would later find out that people were intentionally misleading me about that situation because the people who were allegedly responsible for the act were serving up the city, and many people were invested with the guy directly and indirectly. I was attempting to address something personal and the streets were focused on business. In retrospect I can understand that was the only situation around in a drought, nevertheless when there's something worth putting your title on the line for, you must do it. If your title gets taken, you must trust you will be able to get along without it. The cage or the grave is the consequence of the get back.

During this time **I** started to question some things that weren't making any sense to me. **I** would venture up North Philly to trap street and talk with the big homie. One day I was feeling depressed about "B's" situation and I was deep in my feelings. I explained my history with "B" and how we used to do back flips on dirty mattresses. He replied "I understand how you feel about that, however, you need to be mindful of your own situation. You are new to these streets and you don't have the knowledge of all the players"... He told me that the shit was deeper than rap! Additionally, he told me to stop asking questions about that situation to the people around me because people like to pass messages for a check. He warned me of the impending betrayal that I would suffer if I continued to move around the city in my feelings about situations that occurred long before my release from prison. He warned me about the secret relationships that people had and how certain people had eyes all over the city courtesy of the money bag. He told me the game was dark and slick, if I was going to survive I would need to learn the relationships that guys had cultivated over the years before I could move against someone with that much money. I valued those conversations because he opened my eyes to the dangers of the city. When a real savage thinker has a safe full of money anyone that's attempting to move against him on pure heart and principal doesn't stand a chance!

If the streets are forced to choose between principality and a money bag the graveyards around the world are going to be filled with a bunch of men who stood on principality! "Here lies a good man who thought he meant more to the streets than a money bag." I truly understand that double talking leads to the double cross. As much as I wanted to be real and move on principality the guy standing next to me wanted money and power. The streets are cunning, cruel and heartless. Every time I left trap street I had chills and goose bumps. If your money isn't right the streets will treat you like you're nothing, and if you have the money and don't understand the politics of the city someone is going to trick you out of your position and possibly your life.

I was learning the streets all over again, the old heads gave me a sense of clarity on that issue. He forced me to see the connections that were invisible to me, through the years I've remained faithful to that process, it's part of my nervous system and I apply it to all social situations seeing deeper into others and anticipating their feelings without the need for words. I guess every moment of my life is a line for my obituary.

CHAPTER 20

The Run and The Arrest

After my significant other became a cooperating witness against me she was arrested and incarcerated on a parole violation because the Philadelphia Homicide detectives ran with a story that I was going to murder her if she was released. Up until then I had no idea that she was the witness testifying against me, I was still clueless about her secret relationship with the government. Nevertheless, I was still moving around attempting to secure the funds for her defense when I found out through an attorney that she was the star witness against me and at that time a possible F.B.I. informant. I had already given her cousin my watch to sell, valued at ($12,000); however they never sold it. Instead she called home from jail and instructed them not to sell the watch, but to give it to her brother. My little brothers from my neighborhood seen him with it on and made him take it off.

Meanwhile the S.W.A.T. team is raiding every low key spot I had access to and I'm wondering how they knew so much, I would later learn the woman had given the detectives written permission to access her cell phone account and they had tracked all of my movements from the very first day she gave me the phone. Unbeknownst to me the woman had gave me a hot phone the very first day I was released from prison, she activated the family locator and that phone history was how the police determined which places I would likely go to stay underneath their radar.

I also had a cell phone number registered in her cousin's name, she had given the detectives that phone number as well. Her cousin was hauled in for questioning but she didn't cooperate. She didn't lie either, she gave the police access to her telephone records also. That information was used to raid more houses. The police also subpoenaed my jail house visiting listand raided every address listed. I was cut off from any possible assistance, so I turned to Jazz, my teenage sweetheart. However, I didn't know she was the target of a federal indictment for stealing prescription pads from her job at the hospital. Jazz' brother was arrested in a tri-state sting operation that the Feds were running and he flipped on her. Jazz allowed me to stay at her friends house until I could get out of the city. About two days later Jazz was acting strange whispering on the phone and avoiding eye contact with me. Around 2:00 that afternoon she went to the store and when she came back the S.W.A.T. team was with her. Everyone thought it was her friend "K" that turned me in because I was arrested in her house, but it was Jazz the whole time. She claimed she was going back to the car to get the drinks because she couldn't carry everything at once but she never did come back into the house. It was impossible to have gotten off of the block because the police had everything in a two block radius cornered off and when they finally did get me the police said "you should find better women"... he was referring to the wife and the girlfriend. I guess I was sleeping with my enemies the entire time I was free. No matter whose company I'm in or what they can take away from me I will never exploit a loved ones vulnerability. The biggest mistake I made was not moving when that little voice inside told me to.

I never think of myself as a victim because if I did I would have difficulty trusting myself or anyone else for that matter. When you are a victim you will have someone else to blame for what went wrong and is going wrong in your life. Sure people crossed me who claimed to have loved me, but that was then, this is a new time. There is never a need to prove I made the right choices and am unjustly receiving the wrong results. I'm hated for what I represent, so I can never be loved for who other's want me to be.

CHAPTER 21

Ignorance of the Law

Many men and women have become rats because they are un-educated in the ways of the system. The prosecutor and the police turn people because they can get them to believe that they are in a lot more trouble than they actually are and that kind of deceptive creation is permissible and does not exceed the boundary. The courts have agreed that the police may use what they call **"artifice and strata-gem"** to find criminal activity. So it's perfectly legal for the cops to tell you we are going to take the kids and charge you with a crime "if you don't tell us what we want to know". Your arrest may be illegal but the tactics they use to make you a rat are not, because you do not have a constitutional right to be saved from your own ignorance. Cops and prosecutors are agents of the government. They are not our lawyers and we should never talk to them without a lawyer present. It's a cop's dream to get you alone in an interview room because he can walk all over your constitutional right to a lawyer under the Sixth Amendment. Again ignorance of the law is no excuse! In the cop's and prosecutor's mind you and your kids are a means to justify the end of your mother or father, sister or brother, uncle or aunt, boyfriend or husband, and in some cases even your own sons and daughters! If you are running around in the communities with the pole and trappin then you should at least know what laws you are breaking. As well you should also have the <u>brains</u> to ask for a lawyer when you find yourself in trouble whatever gender you are The ignorance of one person can take down an entire neighborhood.

The United States Supreme Court, THE HIGHEST COURT IN AMERICA has ruled that prosecutors have broad discretion in determining what crimes to investigate and prosecute, and in most cases neither probable cause nor reasonable suspicion is necessary prior to the police doing undercover work. That means when a RAT identifies you as a potential target for investigation, only the most outrageous government conduct violates due process. How "outrageous" can the government be? There is no violation when a RAT has sex with you, because you are a suspect. The RAT can even get high with you, because the Supreme Court has permitted the use of deceit by assuming fake identities to convince you that they are real. The government can supply some ingredients for your drugs, and secretly recruit family members to inform on you and the rest of your family and friends. And to top it all off, the Supreme Court has given the prosecutors and the cops, absolute immunity for all that they do! So anyone can be an informant and you can be arrested, prosecuted, convicted, and imprisoned solely on the sword of someone who you would never suspect. Ratting has become a business, the parole board has a department for informants that are out on parole. The guy who you did jailtime with and you thought was cool, will turn you over to the parole agents for money and/or because he/she is ignorant of the law and the . powers that be has convinced them that they stand to lose something valuable.

The cops make the community think they are serving the greater good, but its a trade-off, they sacrifice the ignorant just to accomplish things. Just remember federal prosecutors are appointed--or, at the state level, elected-to put the alleged bad actor in jail. They need to show the world trophies of their work. At the end of the day its all politics. They use your own ignorance and/or arrogance against you. If you're not careful you will be far from your city in a lonely and cold cell. The mentally strong will fight for their freedom, and the ones who truly have shit for brains will lay down and die off of misery and psychotropic meds, victims of continued • ignorance.

In other words stop hiding drugs in your mother's house, stop putting cars in her name, because when the people come for you, State or Fed, they will be using the love you have for your mother 'against you. In most cases they will tell you to plead guilty or the drugs and Money found at your mother's house will become hers. They will also scare your mother into telling on you. Men only trust their mothers, wives, girlfriends, and sisters. Likewise we will protect them with our lives literally and that only helps the government's case. Sometimes when they come to our houses they only have a body warrant, (they are looking for someone), but they find drugs and/or a gun. They use that to scare people into giving them more information. By the time the ignorant person stops talking, they've told on people who have absolutely nothing to do with the situation. Then they put them on the stand in front of everyone. How do people in the hood know who told on someone, because the police use them up and throw them right back to the wolves with no protection.

—

If you want to know something about the law, just ask an attorney about your rights, your basic rights under the law. But never let your ignorance, or the arrogance of some other ignorant person get you caught up into the treacherous and unforgiving American legal system. In the end, by learning what you're up against you set the stage for yourself and your loved ones to make the right choices that create good. opportunities. Anything else is just other people's perception of reality, and that has nothing to do with your life. There's no such thing as a fair fight when you're ignorant.

CHAPTER 22

—— ✦ ——

The Neighborhood Hate

After the arrest on the murder charge the clowns in my neighborhood were celebrating, I heard things like "that's good for him, they finally got him for good, they are going to put him on death row this time etc." Because of my reputation people had pre-judged me and without the benefit of any evidence. I was convicted in the court of public opinion on the word of an F.B.I. informant along with corrupt Philadelphia Detectives (After my arrest and conviction the lead detective on my case along with ten others were indicted on corruption charges and/or removed from the Homicide Division); if the public chatter was any indication of how I would fair at trial I knew things would get much worse before it would get any better. Most of the time when people are ignorant to the particulars surrounding a situation but continuously speak against someone or something with passion they are working some kind of an angle that requires the support of a specific group of people, the police or a person's street opposition

The intentional assassination of a person's character is an act of war without bloodshed. The challenge with defending against that kind of creative information is distinguishing the gossip from the secret hate. In my case it was the hatred that fueled the neighborhood smear campaign. All of the people who were forced to absorb my presence were hard at work perpetuating lies and attempting to undermine my character, they were spreading half truths about my case which made it a whole lie when people repeated the story. The theory behind that tactic was to kill off any would be supporters, the only way I could defend myself from a position of powerlessness was to share those guys secrets. I started to expose guy's homosexual activities when they were in prison, I exposed some people as rats as well as guys being undercover crackheads. I reminded those guys of who they really were and the smear campaign grinded to a I hated to fight like that but my name is all that I have and I will, protect it with everything inside of me.

Those *guys* are what I call passive aggressive ghetto cowards, they fear direct confrontation with real strength. However their narcissism has a way of overriding reality. They had no idea that strength could become a weakness when abused. The power game can be played with skill, money, or fearlessness. In my experience all three can save a man's character and integrity from lies because sincerity is something real men feel, The frauds feel nothing except hate.

Those people attempted to denigrate my character and portray me as an ignorant corner boy with an insatiable lust for blood. Since I couldn't rely onthe so called "real ones" to challenge the clowns on mybehalf, I addressed the issue the only way I could under the circumstances. I trusted the world, my world would understand the depth of my perspective. I will never allow cowards to change the meaning of strength into an image of weakness in order to disguise their own flaws. A vulture's nature is to prey on the vulnerability of another in hopes of generating a new narrative depicting them as the heroes, understanding that the influence of numbers can compel an entire neighborhood to abandon a person despite history. No words can give me back what I believe was taken from me. I'm not open to love for those kinds of characters because nothing they have to offer will be fulfilling to me. I can celebrate my journey in the streets because I've done nothing to violate that code. To be a man is to be recognized by "the men"; and if you wish to be respected by "the men", even at your weakest, defend your name from the vultures at all cost.

Humor me while I tell you a little parable about oil and water. Can you define a slick guy and a slimy woman? Can you tell the difference between a smirk and a sneer? Among other uses and purposes, water can be used for cleaning, but it also needs to be cleaned up as well. Reason is, if you allow it to sit and fester on a surface for too long it has a tendency to mutate, emerging as a SLIMY substance that ultimately becomes nothing except bacteria and parasites. Don't get me wrong. We need water to live, and it is extremely useful. But if you're not careful, water can and will kill you.

Oil possesses a characteristic known as viscosity, a quality that makes it SLICK to the touch. Among other purposes this makes it quite useful for the functionality of machinery and things of that sort, depending on the type of oil of course.

Now, water moves freely and constantly, by any available means, due to its viscosity, oil not so much. What separates the two is density. Density relates to thickness but can also be thickheadedness. Of the two, oil is clearly the more dense. Pour both substances in a glass and observe. Watch as the oil rises to the top. So back to the topic at hand. SLICK ass oil, or thickheadedness double as arrogance in the form of an individual. As a result, just like oil serves to lubricate whatever kinks in a chain. SLICK guy's motive is to get by utilizing the same approach, the efforts, energies and abilities of other people.

Now let us consider disloyal water. It possesses no permanent shape, for it conforms to the mold or shape that contains it for the moment. Water is very crafty and adaptable. When exposed to frigid temperatures it becomes ice, however, once warmed up it returns to its original form. When exposed to excessive heat it boils and evaporates, transforming into steam, which if captured and cooled regenerates into water again. Think about sitting on the dock of some lake. The water is damned and still, the epitome of patience. This picture can be quite settling and relaxing. At last, what have we learned about the tendencies of water? It festers! Any expert will certainly advise you not to drink it. Little does one realize that quietly beneath the surface water is diligently in search of the path of least resistance. Does it sound familiar? All it requires is the slightest breach in your barrier and the darn will burst. Transforming water from the life source (Friendship/Relationship) into the force of devastation and destruction that it can be. Water don't mind putting in the work because it can take any form at whatever time at whatever place, water plays the long game just like people around you. Ironically, both oil and water can produce a slippery surface, but the two don't mix at all. So my advice to you is to learn the difference between a smirk and a sneer. It will serve to help distinguish between those Slick guys and Slimy women. The end...

Postscript

～

The JBM (Junior Black Mafia) was a group of men from Philadelphia who reigned supreme in the mid 80's to the very early part of the 1990's. Most of the group were friends before and during their reign, but money, greed, women and miscommunication severed a neighborhood bond and in some cases a real childhood bond. Along the way they raised the author as a son, little brother and protege. They taught <u>him</u> how to conduct himself in the mean Philly streets. They dressed him, taught him how to fight, showed him how to hustle and instilled in him a strong neighborhood pride. The author has chosen to touch on an are long gone but it is forever relevant because of the historical street value and its lesson. In many cases the government, Federal and State, has portrayed the members of the JBM as gun toting sociopaths on a mission to murder and flood the black community with crack cocaine. However, what the government failed to mention were that these men were fathers, active fathers that held down real jobs (i.e.) youth counselors in juvenile facilities, Septa bus drivers, Olympic boxing prospects, military personnel, college basketball stars and the list goes on. Good gifts, sometimes come in bad packages! No one is claiming sainthood. However, the label of bloodthirsty marauders is an over the top mischaracterization of the men in question. The label is decades old and out dated. The truth is always available but not perpetuated. The big lie as told by the government and the rats can never be spoken amongst the people who know the truth. If you decide to take a moment to investigate you will see all those life sentences were a product of the name JUNIOR BLACK MAFIA..., but their family and friends are a product of them. The unindicted coconspirators as well as the men who served decades in prison and are now free have the real story available. No more government lies! In addition to what has happened to them it will not end unless the rampant ignorance of the American Justice System is continuously exposed for what itA Politicians playground where "quid pro quo" is the ultimate law!

Acknowledgements...

First off, I want to thank a very special person, "Rashidah" you give me motivation and your patience with me is legendary! Without you this first book doesn't get done and for that I thank u very deeply and I promise to never take your presence in my life for granted! Thank you for accepting me as I am and I vow to always protect your name and image from embarrassment! Secondly, to my old head and father figure D.B. thank you for encouraging me to keep writing and for always treating me like a son! Your wisdom is more than appreciated and I hope to always make u proud! To Gump my old head and big brother thanx for all the love and knowledge your support keeps me strong because steel sharpens steel! To my mother simply put you are my Queen! Uncle L, To my brother, Dad would've been proud to see us together as men don't ever doubt my love for you and thanx for the support! To my three sisters K, L and C even though we are not as close as we used to be I'm still one of yall biggest fans! And to all the bros. in the jail who told me I had a gift thanx for the inspiration!!!

"Dedications".....

I dedicate this book to the entire group of old heads because I learned how to conduct myself in the streets and in life just by being amongst y'all even those that went out sad! Because at one point they had something beneficial to offer! jaymo, slama, Lil Buck (R.I.P.), littles, Rock, Magic, Gump, Manny (R.I.P.), Dirty Black, Storm, Mus (R.I.P.), Mont, Clint (R.I.P.), Ly, Sug, Neal (R.I.P.), Lil E (R.I.P.), Peezo, B-bop and some others who asked me not to mention their names. Can't forget Mars, Black Mally, D-Man (R.I.P.), Ed starks, tippy, Fat Juice, Ted, Sonny, tatmoe and so many others! My big brothers, Lil Ben, Dre Mason, Stevie G, Markese, A.P., Sleep, Lil Ern, (R.I.P), Tone Beff, Cory Mac, Darwin, and there's a few more...And my friends that still look back Fat Malik, L.A., Dro, My ill bro. The twins from P street, Goob, big brother dedications Ceaser, Tall D (R.I.P.), KENNY 60TH St.(R.I.P.) Daunte aka Namo (R.I.P.) and put this in the homie section, Snake, Ty-yell (RIP.), Buttons (R.I.P.) Johnny Coo-coo (R.I.P.), Fly Ty, little Malik

Zay from the "0" Dame, Z.B. Malik Mill, P.W. and K.B. if I forgot u and your relevant in my life please forgive me. The Southwest that I used to know and the one currently being held down by the real ones and of course THE ENTIRE WOODLAND AVENUE OLD HEADS BECAUSE Y'ALL MADE IT SAFE FOR EVERYONE!!!

Lightning Source UK Ltd.
Milton Keynes UK
UKHW051105200422
401735UK00006B/404

9 798985 869590